Printed in Great Britain
by Amazon

80993399R10032